THE SUN DANCE
OF THE
BLACKFOOT INDIANS

BY

CLARK WISSLER

Preface.

The Blackfoot tribes, particularly the Piegan, have been more extensively studied than most other Plains Indians. The writer began a systematic investigation of their culture in 1903. At that time, the only works treating them seriously were those of the younger Henry, Maximilian, and Grinnell. There were some good fragmentary articles by McLean and Hale. Yet, since we began work on this problem, a number of excellent books have appeared. First, the long-forgotten journals of Mathew Cocking and Anthony Hendry who went to the Blackfoot country in 1754 were printed. Then followed McClintock's delightful book, "The Old North Trail" and later, Curtis's highly illustrated account of the Piegan. Linguistic studies had been undertaken by Tims, but later, Michelson, Uhlenbeck, and Josselin de Jong brought out studies of the language and some aspects of social organization. Of more popular books, the only one to be considered here is Schultz's, "My Life as an Indian," which, though in the form of fiction, is full of true pictures of Blackfoot life and thought. One unfortunate thing about all this subsequent activity is that it centered on the Piegan and as the writer's work was largely with that division before these publications appeared, there was no chance to rectify this asymmetry.

The publication of this study of the sun dance has been long delayed in the hope that circumstances would permit a more intensive study of the ceremony among the Canadian divisions. But the time for making such a study has really passed, since those natives who had the knowledge essential to an accurate exposition of the sun dance are now dead. It seems advisable, therefore, to publish the data as they stand.

The writer saw the Piegan ceremony twice, so that this study is based both upon objective observation and discussion with the native authorities on the subject. Later, Mr. Duvall checked over the data and conclusions with these and other informants. A large series of photographs was taken, but the important phases of the ceremony are so well shown in the published works of McClintock and Curtis that a repetition here is unnecessary.

Clark Wissler.

May, 1918.

The Sun Dance.

In our earlier paper upon the bundles of the Blackfoot, we have concerned ourselves with ceremonial functions in which the ownership and chief responsibility, in theory, rested in a single individual. We come now to an affair initiated, it is true, by the owner of the natoas bundle, but yet a composite of other rituals and functions, each of which has a definite place in a program carried out by the whole tribal organization. The only trace of a similar tribal participation is in the now almost extinct tobacco-planting ceremonies conducted by the beaver owners; but here there was no complex of other unrelated ceremonies and functions. In short, the sun dance was for the Blackfoot a true tribal festival, or demonstration of ceremonial functions, in which practically every important ritual owner and organization had a place. Nevertheless, there were certain rituals peculiar to it which gave it its character.

Since the plan of this section is to give an ethnological presentation of the Blackfoot sun dance, rather than a logically unfolding description of the ceremony as seen at a specified time, we shall present the general program now and take up later a somewhat analytical detailed discussion of the various phases of the ceremony. By this method, we shall be able to concentrate our attention upon a single ceremonial concept without the distraction arising from contemporaneous and intrusive procedures based upon other concepts, for as we shall see, this sun dance is a true composite. The following schedule is not given as the one observed by the writer, but as the one regarded as proper and believed to have been followed before the various divisions of the Blackfoot were under the complete domination of the Canadian and United States governments.

Preparation Period.

After making a vow to purchase a sun dance bundle, the woman and her husband make the necessary arrangements and perform the prescribed rites. This is an indefinite period. At the approach of summer, the invitation tobacco is sent to all the bands and the camp circle is formed.

Program by Days.

First Day.

The program opens with moving camp to a site previously selected. On the morning of this day, the medicine woman begins to fast, which may be taken as the real beginning of the ceremony. If the ceremony of "cutting the tongues" has not been previously performed or completed, it is now in order. In any event, the father and any male assistants he may choose to invite, spend a part of the day in "praying and singing over the tongues." A society brings in willows and a hundred-willow sweathouse is built.

Second Day.

In the morning, the camp moves again to a site still nearer that proposed for the sun dance. A few green boughs of cottonwood are kept around the base of the medicine woman's tipi as a sign of its sanctity. A sweathouse is made, as on the previous day. "Praying and singing over the tongues" continues during the day and evening.

Third Day.

The same as the second day.

Fourth Day.

The camp moves again; this time to the site of the sun dance. In the afternoon, the fourth and last hundred-willow sweathouse is built and used. The singing continues during the evening in the medicine woman's tipi.

Fifth Day.

This is an active day.[1] The various bands cut and drag in the poles and green cottonwood boughs to be used in constructing the dancing lodge. The center, or sun pole, is selected and brought in with the ceremonies pertaining thereto. During the day, the holes for the posts are dug and the sides of the dancing lodge put in place and prepared for the raising at sunset. A wind-break is erected at the west side, facing the forked end of the sun pole. Later in the day, some medicinemen take up their stations here to receive offerings to the sun and place them on the pole. In the forenoon, the ceremony connected with the opening of the natoas bundle begins in the medicine woman's tipi. This is completed by the middle of the afternoon when there is a procession from the tipi to the wind-break facing the sun pole. The thongs for the poles are cut. While these are taking place, some food is distributed among the poor people. Those women, who, during the past season, promised "to come forward to the tongues" now fulfil their vows by public declarations addressed to the setting sun. The pole raisers then approach from the four quarters, erecting first the sun pole and then the rafters, with as much speed as possible. The medicine woman then returns to her tipi and the father with his male companions goes into a sweathouse.

Sixth Day.

In the morning, a booth is erected in the dancing lodge for the medicinemen, or weather dancers. Later in the day, they approach, with processions made up of their respective bands, and take their places in the booth. At various times during the day, they dance to the sun. People also come up to be painted and prayed for. As a rule, the medicine-pipes are brought out for these men to bless

---

[1] As in many other cases, there is a difference of opinion as to what was, or is, the correct schedule. Some maintain that the timber and sun pole are brought in on the fourth day and the fifth day given over to the erection of the dancing lodge only. This is, however, a matter of no great moment.

and smoke. During the afternoon, the "digging dance" occurs, when the fireplace is made and the fire kindled.

Seventh Day.

People still come to be painted or prayed for by the medicinemen. Later in the day, the dancing of the societies begins.

Eighth Day.

The dancing may continue on this day; otherwise, camp is broken and the bands go their several ways. The dancing may continue several days, there being no definite time for closing the ceremony. Indeed, to the Blackfoot mind, the really vital part of the ceremony closes on the evening of the fifth day. The dancing of the societies is free to take its course as the various organizations see fit. In former times, however, it was customary to break camp any time between the seventh and tenth days.

According to our information, the four camps of the medicine woman was the rule in olden times and a hundred-willow sweathouse was made at each camp. In recent times, but two moves seem to have been made; the first day marking the move from the regular home camp to the temporary one where the second day is also spent. But one of the hundred-willow sweathouses is now made—the one on the third day. Also, where formerly they used the ordinary type of sweathouse, at the close of the fourth day, the men now return to the hundred-willow sweathouse. The time then was "when the service berries are ripe", perhaps August, instead of Fourth-of-July week, as in recent years.[2] Even the fast is much abbreviated, usually but of two days' duration.

---

[2] See Grinnell, George Bird, *Blackfoot Lodge Tales* (New York, 1903), 264, for program.

The Vow.

The most important functionary in the Blackfoot sun dance is a woman, known among the whites as the medicine woman, and upon a clear comprehension of her functions and antecedents depends our understanding of the ceremony itself. Accordingly, we shall proceed with as complete an exposition of her office as the information at hand allows. In the first place, a sun dance cannot occur unless some woman qualifies for the office. On the other hand, it was almost inconceivable that there should be a summer in which such a qualification would not be made. This attitude of our informants implies that public opinion had sufficient force to call out volunteers against their own wills. There was a feeling that an annual sun dance was, from a religious and ethical point of view, necessary to the general welfare, for which some individual ought to sacrifice personal comfort and property to the extent required by custom. As we shall see later, this was no small price to pay for a doubtful honor. This feeling was sure to express itself in the subtle ways peculiar to Indian society, if need be, to the direct suggestion of a candidate who in turn felt impelled to come forward as if prompted entirely from within.

As a rule, however, the woman qualifies by a vow. Oftimes, when a member of the family is dangerously ill, one of the women goes out of the tipi and raising her eyes to the sun calls upon it that health may be restored to the ailing one. In such an appeal she offers to make gifts to the sun, usually specifying that she will sacrifice a piece of cloth, a dress, a robe, an ax, etc., which are after a time, provided the sick one improves, hung in trees or deposited upon a hill. Such appeals are still made with great frequency. It is believed that unless the woman has been industrious, truthful, and above all, true to her marriage vows, her appeal will not be answered. Sometimes, when the woman addresses the sun she promises to be the medicine woman at the next sun dance. She herself may be ill and promise such a sacrifice in case she receives help. Again, she may, out of gratitude for the satisfactory way in which her prayers have been answered, announce her intention to take this step. In such a case, a formal announcement is made to the sun. In company with a man, usually a medicineman experienced in the ceremonies, she steps out into the camp, where they face the sun whom the man addresses, explaining that as this woman asked for help in time of need and that inasmuch as it was granted, she in turn promises to be the medicine woman at the first opportunity. Some such formal announcement is made in every case where the prayers have been answered. By this formality, the vow receives public registry.

As indicated above, the prayers are not always granted. In such cases, the promises are not only not binding, but to proceed with the sun dance, or to take a secondary part in it, would be to the detriment of all concerned. The fault is said to lie in the woman's life and that only the wrath of the sun would be invoked by her participation in the ceremonies.

It may be asked if a man can make such a vow. He may and does often call upon the sun, promising gifts of property or even scalps and may promise to furnish the material support for a wife, mother, sister, or in fact any woman who will come forward to perform the ceremony. Thus, a Blood chief once told us that he had been very ill all winter; that he had tried all kinds of doctors without relief, until he was stripped of all his property. At last, he recovered and then made a vow that with the help of his wife he would give the sun dance. This he did, but, as he expressed it, "with great difficulty because he was then poor and did not receive adequate help from his relatives."

Again, it must be noted that women who do not feel equal to the responsibility of the medicine woman's office, make a vow to announce publicly their virginity or faithfulness to their marriage vows, as the case may be, though for an unmarried woman to make such a pledge is the exception. This is spoken of as "the going forward to the tongues," the full meaning of which will appear later. The manner and occasion of making this vow are in most respects similar to the preceding. At a certain stage of the sun dance proceedings, all the women who made such a promise to the sun, come forward and make their statements subject to the challenge of any man present. This bears some resemblance to the virginity tests of the Dakota, but applies more particularly to married women and marital virtue than otherwise.

Naturally, the number of women making promises of this kind was much greater than for the more important ceremony. Thus, we have a custom of calling upon the sun in time of need which is an almost universal practice, a more restricted form of such appeal peculiar to women in so far that sexual morality is a necessary qualification, the more specific vow of "going forward to the tongues", and the exceptional vow to perform the medicine woman's functions at the sun dance, a fair illustration of the way in which most complex folk ceremonies are supported by a pyramid of less and less differentiated practices.

In passing, it should be noted that when the vow is made to perform the medicine woman's functions, it is literally an obligation to purchase a natoas bundle, or if already the owner of a bundle, to perform its ritual.[3] A woman may own more than one of these bundles at a time; indeed, we have heard of a woman purchasing new ones at several successive sun dances. This purchase is a fundamental feature in all bundle ceremonies to which the sun dance bundle offers no exception.

On the other hand, the vow means more than the mere purchase of a bundle. We are told that the requirement as to virtue holds strictly for the vow and the tongue ceremony. A woman can buy a natoas in the ordinary sense and have it transferred with the ritual

---

[3] This series, volume 7, 215.

even though she has not been true to her husband. We are reminded that Scabby-round-robe's wife[4] was not true to her former husband and that when her husband received a beaver bundle there went with it a natoas and accessories; but that while she could use them by virtue of her relation to a beaver bundle, she was not competent to make a vow and initiate a sun dance.[5] This is consistent with the tradition that the natoas was once bought from a beaver bundle by a woman who gave the sun dance for that year and used instead of a wreath of juniper as in former ceremonies. It also throws some light on the relation of the natoas to the beaver and the sun dance rituals.

---

[4] This series, vol. 2, 83.

[5] For example, we were told that some few years ago the widow of Spotted-eagle took the part of the medicine woman and borrowed a natoas from the mother of Curly-bear. Recently (1911), the latter died. Then the former claimed the natoas on the grounds that she had paid full value for it at the time and that she had now the most right to it. Curly-bear consented. Then, after an interval, this woman transferred it to the wife of —— who made no vow to give the sun dance, for it was generally known that the reputation of the new owner permanently disqualified her for the function of medicine woman.

Ceremony of the Tongues.

While it is obvious from the preceding, that the medicine woman takes her vow at no fixed period in the year, the order of procedure is such that as a rule, she must have taken her vow not later than the spring of the year in which the sun dance occurs. There is no absolute prohibition to qualifying at a later time, as is often the case at present when the consent of the Indian Agent must be obtained before the ceremony is permitted, but the normal order seems to be as just stated. Any way, in the spring, the medicine woman calls upon her relatives for buffalo tongues (in recent years, those of cattle). These are then saved as requested. In passing, it may be noted that in all ceremonies, the persons upon whom the burden of responsibility falls have not only an inherent right to call upon their blood relatives, but these in turn are under obligations to respond. The number of tongues required is uncertain, some informants claiming that there should be an even hundred, others, that four to five full parfleches was the standard. Naturally, in recent years, the number has been much less. These tongues are to be sliced, parboiled, and dried like meat. The slices, however, must be perfect, without holes, and come from the interior of the tongue.

The slicing of these tongues appears to have been the first ceremony of the cycle. It is conducted by a man, usually the father, who formally announced the woman's vow and who conducts all the ceremonies in which the medicine woman takes part. There is no stipulation that the same man must direct all parts of the ceremony, but, by custom, this office is performed annually by the same man so long as he is physically capable. To this ceremony are called the medicine woman, the women who have promised to "go forward to take the tongues", and sometimes those having previously performed these functions.

The manner of formally registering the vow and of collecting the tongues is stated as follows:—

Now the woman who made the vow calls on a man and woman who have been through the medicine lodge ceremony to announce it. The man and woman come to her tipi and paint her clothes and face and those of the relative for whom the vow was made with red paint. Prayers are offered for them and a few songs sung. After this, the four stand in front of the tipi and the man announces the vow. He says, "Sun, she is going to make a sun lodge for you. I think you and those who are above can hear what is said." Then they move in turn to the south, west, and north side of the tipi, repeating the same words at each stop and finally enter the tipi.

In the spring of the year, when the people run buffalo, the woman has her tipi a little towards the front or center. It may be that she is only with one of the bands, while the rest are camped elsewhere. Her tipi stands alone a little to the west of the others. The people are then notified that the tongues are to be given to the woman. Her husband mounts his horse and sets out, taking a pipe and tobacco, but no weapons with him. When he finds a man butchering, he sits down on a robe, fills his pipe, prays for those present, and smokes with them. The butcher cuts out the tongue, wipes it off with sagegrass, and places it near the man, who has spread some buffalo dung with sagegrass on top of it in a row before him. The tongues are placed on the sage and dung. The man then takes the tongues and rides to where the next man is butchering and goes through the same procedure. After he has gathered up all the tongues he takes them home. Each time buffalo are killed the man rides out to gather in tongues until he has accumulated a hundred.

The tongues having been collected, an important ceremony follows with their boiling and slicing. An experienced man and woman are invited to direct; these are spoken of as the father and the mother. Also, all the women having made a vow "to go forward to the tongues" are invited. In addition, a number of women and men familiar with the ceremonies are called. The woman making the vow (the daughter) and her husband (the son) sit at the back of the fire; next to the former, sits the mother and then the other women; next to the latter, sits the father and then the men in order. The men sit on the north side and the women on the south. At the proper moment, the mother brings in the tongues, passing around to the south side, and lays them in rows on a half rawhide back of the fire. All the women having made vows are now called upon to slice the tongues. Their husbands must be present.

The tongues are slit open and the women are invited to slice and boil them. When all the guests are present, one of the tongues is taken and painted black on one edge and red on the other, and given to the woman who made the vow. The rest of the tongues are handed to the women for skinning and slicing; if there were more tongues than women, each was given more than one to slice. After all the women have the tongues, the woman with the painted tongue makes a confession, saying, "Sun, I have been true to my husband ever since I have been with him and all my life. Help me, for what I say is true. I will skin this tongue without cutting a hole in it or cutting my fingers."

The next woman also makes a confession, and so on. After all have confessed, they commence to skin the tongues. As the first woman takes up the knife, the song runs: "A sharp thing I have taken; it is powerful." The knife is painted, one half red, the other black. Should any of the women cut a hole in the tongue skin or cut their fingers, it is a sign that they must have lied and they are ordered from the tipi. At the outset, each woman carefully examines her tongue to see if the skin is perfect. Should a hole be found, the tongue is passed to the director who marks it with black paint. After the tongues are all skinned and sliced, they are passed back to the woman who distributed them and placed in a wooden bowl. The skins of the tongues are tied in bunches with sinew so that they can tell to which woman the skins belong.

The skins are to be boiled by two women. Two sticks are given to one woman and one to the other. All this time singing is going on. The woman who has the two sticks paints them black, while the woman who has the other, paints it red. The three sticks are tied together at one end and are used as a tripod for hanging the kettle in which the skins of the tongues are to be boiled. The legs of the tripod, the wooden kettle hook, and all other sticks are painted half in red and half in black. Also, the kettle is marked with four vertical bands of black and four of red. The four blunt sticks for stirring the pot are painted in pairs, red and black. A red and black painted stick is slipped through the bail, passed around to the north of the tipi, and handed to the two women. During all these movements there is praying and singing. The women each take hold of one end of the stick and go for water.

They make four pauses on this journey, each time praying to the sun and asserting their marital rectitude and recounting such occasions as they have been improperly approached by a man. All this time, the father and his assistants sing in the tipi. One of the women takes a cup, makes four movements with it and dips the water. At this moment the song runs:—

"The water that I see. Water is sacred."

On the return, the women make four pauses as before. When the pail is finally within the tipi, incense is burned between the fireplace and the door and the pail held in the smudge. The father takes up the board upon which some of the tongues lie and while holding it up in one hand, shakes the cup about in the water, meanwhile making a noise like the buffalo, finally striking the pail a blow with the cup. Here the song runs:—

"Buffalo will drink."

This may be taken as marking one stage of the ceremony. The boiling of the tongue is now in order. When all is ready, the father starts the songs in the next series. The two women hook the kettle on the tripods and while the kettle is heated, there are other songs and incense burned and the song runs:—

"Where I (buffalo speaking) sit is sacred."

While the water boils, the director takes up a tongue, holds it above the kettle, lowers it slowly, making a noise as if something were drinking. After this, the women place the tongues in the kettle and proceed with the boiling. Here or elsewhere, songs accompany the ceremonial acts. The pot must not boil over.

When the tongues have cooked, the two women rise and stand by the fire as the songs begin. At the proper moment, they remove the kettle and place it on the spot where the smudge was made. First, they take out the painted tongues and then the others. The father takes up a small piece, singing:—

"Old Man (sun), he wants pemmican. He wants to eat.
Old Woman (moon), she wants back fat. She wants to eat.
Morningstar, he wants broth. He wants to eat."

Then the painted tongue is passed to the daughter. Now, each of the women tears off a bit of the tongue skin and all hold up the pieces and pray. After the prayers, the pieces are placed in the earth and the tongues are hung up to dry. First, the rope is taken up and a song sung. The woman who made the vow, rises and ties one end of the rope to the tipi pole on the north side and the other end to the tipi pole on the south side, a little to the west of the fireplace. All the tongues, both painted and unpainted, are hung on this rope.

During all these ceremonies there is no regular smudge. The smudges are made with sweetgrass on the grass near the rear of the tipi. The tongues are left to hang for two days before they are taken down to be cooked. When the tongues have been hung, all return to their homes, the women taking the tongue skins with them for their relatives to eat, as they are considered to be blessed and supposed to bring good luck.

After two days, all meet again in the same tipi. The two women who went for the water place the tripods over the fire and while songs are sung, the pot is passed to them with the red painted sticks. The two women, each holding one end of the stick, go for water, praying on the way. When they return to the tipi a smudge, over which they hold the bucket of water, is made between the door and the fireplace. Then the bucket is placed beside the smudge. While the others sing, the woman who made the vow rises and first takes the painted tongue and then the others from where they were hung. They are then placed on a buffalo hide and the woman returns to her place. Four women sit down near the tongues; each one takes a tongue, one of which is the painted one. Kneeling and swaying their bodies in time with the songs, they sing the buffalo songs. The painted tongue is placed in the kettle first and a song is sung: "When buffalo go to drink; it is powerful. Where buffalo sit is powerful (natojiwa)." Then the rest of the tongues are placed in the pot which is hooked on the tripod over the fire. Songs are sung and four sticks, about the length of the forearm, for stirring the tongues, are placed where the tongues were first placed. One of the cooks takes a pair of the sticks and stirs the tongues with them. When removing the tongues from the kettle they are held between two of these sticks.

Another song, called the song of rest is sung, and all rest for a time and smoke. When the tongues are cooled, another song is sung, the two cooks rise, and taking the pot, place it over the smudge place near the door. To the singing of songs, the painted tongue first, and then the others, are taken out and placed on half a rawhide. The soup is poured into wooden bowls and distributed among those present. No tin cups must be used in drinking this soup. While all sing, the woman who made the vow rises and first takes the painted tongue and then all the others and hangs them up as before. This ends the ceremony.

Two days later, the same participants are called together to the same tipi and the woman rises and takes first the painted tongue and then the others from where they were hung. A parfleche is brought and a buffalo song sung: "Buffalo I take. Where I sit is powerful." The painted tongue and then the others are placed on the parfleche. Wild peppermint is put in with the tongues, the parfleches are tied up and placed at the rear of the tipi. Sometimes tongues are dried in front of the tipi on a stage made by setting up two travois with a lodge pole tied between them.

The man and woman who lead the ceremony must not have any metal about them. Brass rings, earrings, and all such trinkets must be taken off. Nor must there be any knives in the vicinity. Even the knives with which the tongues are cut are taken out. No one must spit in front of him, but always close to the wall under the beds. If they do, it will rain. No water is brought into the medicine lodge and when water is brought, it is covered. The only time when it is permitted to eat or drink is before sunrise and after sunset. They must be given food by the instructors. The prayers in this ceremony are prayers for good luck for everyone in the camp.

This closes the preliminaries to the ceremonies leading to the sun dance and may be designated as the cutting of the tongues. As in most other cases, there seems to have been considerable variation in this procedure, both as to time and order. Certainly, for a number of years, it has been much abbreviated. As implied in the program, this ceremony may be performed on the first day. The gathering of tongues was dependent upon circumstances and after the days of the great buffalo drives was a matter of gradual accumulation. Thus, it was explained that by necessity, the "cutting" was often repeated, though naturally with less ceremony.

The parfleches containing tongues are kept in the medicine woman's tipi where they are "prayed and sung over" during the first and second days of the program. The underlying thought seems to be that they are consecrated to the sun.

In the procession of the fourth day, the parfleches are carried behind the medicine woman by her attendants. In former years, these were the women who had promised "to go forward to the tongues." They are present at the ceremony in the medicine woman's tipi and may be said to be in attendance during the entire fasting period. At the time indicated in the program, the parfleches are opened and the women in turn step out with some of the dried tongue, face the west, and each holding up a piece, address the sun then nearing the horizon. They declare their innocence of adultery, as at the time of making the vow and cutting the tongues. They also pray for themselves and their relatives after which they distribute dried tongue among them. Finally, there is a general distribution of tongues among the people.

However, there is another aspect of their appearance at this point. The Blackfoot assume that many women have at one or more periods of their lives been invited by a man to commit the offence and that often the occasion is one of great temptation or calls for great presence of mind and will power. Now, when addressing the sun, if so approached, the woman narrates the circumstances, naming the men committing the offence, and recounts the manner of her refusal. In naming the offender, they usually say, "I suppose he hears what I say." These women are also subject to challenge of their having committed adultery. It will be seen from this that the part they take in the ceremony is an ordeal for which most women have little liking and one which they will not undertake lightly. The Blackfoot, themselves, regard it as one of the most solemn occasions in the ceremony. So far as we could learn, no one now living was ever present when one of these women was challenged, but the naming of men who were guilty of improper advances was not unusual.

A retrospect of the concept of the tongues indicates that the entire ceremony, or their association with the medicine woman and those who are sexually pure, gives them a potency that may be acquired by eating. They seem most closely associated with sexual purity since they are less primary in the function of the medicine woman than in case of those who "go forward," the former being required to possess many virtues, the latter but one. While the medicine woman fasts and keeps to her tipi, the others do not.

The Medicine Woman.

We shall now give our attention to the medicine woman. As previously stated, she is in most respects the central figure in the whole ceremony, around whom centers its more serious and solemn aspects. On the fifth day, an elaborate ritual is demonstrated in her tipi, culminating in the procession to the dancing lodge. To this ritual belongs a medicine bundle with accessories, known as the natoas, though the name is primarily that of the headdress which the bundle contains. This bundle is transferred in the ritualistic way to the medicine woman by the ceremony and thus becomes hers to care for and guard until used again at another sun dance ceremony. The ritual and the bundle have been discussed in detail in Volume 7 of this series. In addition to the contents of the bundle, there must be a special robe of elkskin, a dress of the same material, and wristlets of strong elk teeth. A new travois must be provided for moving the medicine woman outfit. Sometimes she herself rides on it. This travois is made by the past medicine woman, her attendant in the ceremonies.

As previously stated, the natoas ritual in the sun dance has for its mythical basis the Elk-woman and the Woman-who-married-a-star, though Scar-face, Cuts-wood, Otter-woman, and Scabby-round-robe are said to have made minor contributions. Versions of these myths may be consulted in Volume 2, part I of this series. The Woman-who-married-a-star is credited with bringing down the digging-stick and the turnip, together with the songs pertaining thereto (p. 61), also a wreath of juniper formerly worn in place of the natoas and the eagle feather worn by the man.

It is also interesting to note that the Crane-woman who transfers the ritualistic attributes of these objects makes a formal declaration of her marital virtue. In the case of Elk-woman, we have again the incident of the Crane and the digging-stick where it is implied that the latter symbolizes the bill of the former. We are informed that many animals were present at this transfer, each contributing something to the regalia. We also find it suggested that the bunches of feathers on the natoas represent the horns of the elk, the elk robe and elk teeth wristlets further symbolizing that animal. In one version of this myth is the antagonistic implication that Elk-woman was not quite up to the standard of marital virtue. In the Cuts-wood myth the "going forward to the tongues" is accounted for. Scabby-round-robe is credited with adding the necklace and the arrow point to the natoas and Otter-woman with the wild cat-tail.

The following statement of an informant has a bearing upon this point:—

The natoas is said to have come from the Elk. It was first owned by beaver bundle men, but it was the custom for the medicine woman in the sun dance to borrow it for her ceremony. This continued for a time, but ultimately the medicine woman bought it and kept it in a bundle of her own. The feathers on the front of the natoas are said to represent the horns of Elk and the plumes at the sides, the leafy top of the large turnip. This is the same turnip which the woman who went to the sky land is supposed to have dug up. The digging-stick which accompanies the natoas also represents the stick with which she did this digging. Some of the songs in the natoas ritual speak of little children running about and this refers to the ball-like image on the front of the natoas, for this image is stuffed with tobacco seeds, which, as you know, are often spoken of as children, or dwarfs (p. 201). The broad band upon which the natoas is mounted is said to represent the lizard. All these things, it is said, were added to the natoas, one at a time, by some of the beaver men. So it came about that we have the natoas as it is.

Now, as to the story about the Elk giving the Natoas the robe and the wristlets used with it. The objection is sometimes made that this first woman who ran away from her husband to join the

Elk was not a true woman and that the facts are therefore inconsistent with the ideal of the natoas ritual. Yet, some of our people claim that the woman was true and that though she went away with the Elk it was merely for the sake of receiving the ritual and that this is evident because in the story it tells how she was able to hook down trees by her magical powers and it is not conceivable that she could do this if she had not been a true woman.

The ceremonial transfer of the sun dance bundle really begins with the fasting of the medicine woman on the first day. Neither she nor her husband are supposed to eat or drink while the sun is visible, and then but sparingly. On the evening before, they are put to bed by the father and mother. The mother places the daughter on the south side of the fire and the father the son on the north side. They must remain in the same position until morning. Before the sun rises the father and mother go to the medicine woman's tipi, stand by the door and sing. They sing as they formally enter, the father raising up the son; the mother, the daughter. The man is taken out by the father and the daughter by the mother for the morning toilet. When they return a small amount of food is fed to the son and daughter, after which the father and mother take a little food and drink. This must be before sunrise. During the day the son and especially the daughter must sit quietly in their places with bowed heads and eyes cast down. She wears a buffalo robe, hair side in, painted red, covering her head as well as her body. Her hair is not braided, but hangs down freely except for a horizontal band around the head. The hair may be allowed to conceal the entire face.

The daughter must do nothing for herself. If she wishes to speak it must be in almost a whisper in the ear of the mother or other attendant, who in turn will announce the import, if necessary. A fire is kept burning in the middle of the tipi, the ears are closely drawn around the smoke hole, the door closed, and the tipi cover securely staked down at the edges. Though this keeps the temperature high, the medicine woman cannot use a fan, but may use the skin of a muskrat to wipe the perspiration from her face and hands.

During the fasting period no noise must be made in the tipi. All the attendants must avoid unnecessary conversation and speak in a very subdued tone; utensils must not be rattled or struck together. Visitors may enter, but respectfully and quietly. No noises should be made in the vicinity of the medicine tipi and boisterous acts abstained from in all parts of the camp circle. If water is brought in the vessel must be covered. No one should spit in the tipi nor do the other things forbidden at the ceremony of the tongues.

Throughout the whole period there is a male attendant. He keeps the fire alive during the night and until camp is moved. He can only start the fire with an ember from some other tipi, striking fire in the tipi being strictly prohibited. Pipes can only be lighted from the fire by this attendant with service berry sticks. A blaze must be avoided as much as possible. The attendant cuts the tobacco and fills the pipe and when burnt out he must empty the ashes into a small hole in the ground near his seat. Everyone is expected to sit quietly, leaving the moving to him. He remains on duty during the night also.

Formerly, the tipi of the medicine woman was moved three times, four different camps resulting, the last being at its position in the circle for the sun dance. As a considerable journey was often necessary to reach the sun dance site these camps might be far apart. Theoretically, the camp is pitched late in the afternoon of each day. At the sun dance a special sweathouse ceremony takes place. This will be discussed later. After this the evening and greater part of the night are spent by those in attendance at the medicine woman's tipi in rehearsing the songs and instructing the son and daughter.

Like everything else, moving the camp of the medicine woman is a formal matter. The travois is made, painted red, and reserved for the special use of the medicine woman. When the time for breaking camp in the medicine woman's band arrives, she and her husband are led out and seated upon a robe at the west or rear of their tipi, facing in the direction to move. The parfleche of tongues and other paraphernalia are brought out by the attending women and put down beside the couple. The mother directs the attending women in taking down the tipi and hitching the horse to the travois. The parfleche of tongues is packed on the travois. When all is ready, the woman and man are led to their horses and assisted to mount, the woman riding the horse to the travois. The father and the son go ahead in single file, next the mother and the daughter, or medicine woman. They pause four times, as songs are sung. After they get some distance out, they stop and wait for the camp, now moving for the first time. This procession of four always leads, the two men side by side and behind them the two women likewise. At noon, when they stop for lunch, the two are again seated on a robe, the travois unhooked and laid down before them. Then follows the camp some distance behind. The old men form a circle and smoke near the pair.

At this time the father orders one of the men's societies to go forward and mark out a camp site. When this spot is reached, tipis are pitched and when everything is in place the medicine woman and her husband are taken inside.

On the morning of each day a society is given instructions to make the sweathouse at the camping place, a man to get the creeping juniper and another to cut out the smudge place. As the sweathouse procedure is a distinct ceremony, it will be treated under another head.

The following account of the evening ceremonies in the medicine woman's tipi was given by Red-plume:—

In the evening, after sunset, the first sweathouse is made. All those who took part in the ceremony before and a few other old men are invited. The man who fills the pipes and tends to the smoking during the ceremony remains on duty during the whole sun dance ceremony. Four-bears is told to tell the mosquito society to sing that night in their own tipi which is inside of the circle. This society is to sing the sun dance songs, the weather-makers dancing songs, the rest of the people remaining quiet through the night. In the medicine lodge they sing until a little before day-break.

The smudge place in the medicine lodge on the first day and for the first sweathouse is a square marked in the soft earth with a crescent in the middle of it. It is not painted. Under the crescent is a dot where the smudge is made.

When all the guests are assembled in the tipi the ceremony for the evening begins. Food is given to all; the medicine woman and her husband have their meat cut up for them. While a song is sung a piece of meat is held over the smudge, four passes made with it, and then fed to the man and woman. The same thing is done with water. After this they may help themselves to the food. After the meal is over the singing begins. The sweetgrass is taken up and a song sung: "Old man, takes spring grass. Old woman comes in with her body." Another man takes the smudge stick and places a live coal on the smudge place. The singer holds the grass over head and then brings it down on the coal. This song is for the morningstar: "Morningstar says let us have a sweathouse." Seven songs are sung for the sun and moon which are spoken of as the old man and old woman. These with the seven sung for the morningstar make fourteen sung thus far.

Since the men have been in the sweathouse where the paint has all washed off, five songs are sung to re-paint the man and woman. As the man sings, he takes some red earth paint with a ball of fat which he rolls in the palms of his hands. The song is: "Old man says red face I take." He makes a streak crosswise on the man's forehead, vertically on his cheeks, and across the chin. The entire face is then covered with the same red paint. The robe is then taken from the man's shoulders. He sings another song as he takes up the sagegrass and brushes one side of the man's head, his arm, and then his body. At the same time, the woman is painted on the other side of the tipi. Another song is sung and he takes the paint, rubs it in his hands, and sings: "This man I am making his body holy, powerful." The same words are sung for the woman. The man's body and robe are then painted.

When the tongues were first taken in to be sliced, two round buffalo dungs together with a ball of sweetgrass were given to the man and woman. They keep these to wipe the paint from their hands. A song is sung for the dung. The two men and the two women hold their hands over the dung. They make four motions with the closed fists and then touch the ground to the southeast, southwest, northwest, and northeast of the dung. The words in this song are: "This may help me to live long, and help me through life." There is also part of a buffalo dung. The smudge stick is taken up, with the song: "Timber I am looking for? Timber I have found and taken." The two men and the two women all grasp the forked stick. They sing as they take up the dung with it and gradually move it up the stick until it rests on the fork. Then it is held over the fire. Someone knocks the dung into the fire and it is covered with ashes. The song is: "Powerful, I start. Powerful where I sit." To throw the dung off into the fire is a sign that enemies will be conquered.

Four songs are now sung for the muskrat skin used to wipe the faces of the man and woman: "Man says, my medicine, I am looking for. I have found it." The skin is taken up. Two songs are sung for the parfleche with tongues in it. It is taken up very slowly and the singing continues during all the movements made with it. It is held over the smudge and placed to one side, the cords untied, and the tongues taken out and distributed to all who are now in the tipi. The two medicinemen and women also eat. The song when first taking up the parfleche is: "Buffalo I am powerfully starting. It is powerful where I sit." When undoing the cords the words are: "Buffalo I take some." When the first tongue is taken out, a little piece is held up by everyone, prayers are said, the small pieces are placed on the ground, and they begin to eat them.

Seven songs for the eagle tail feather with which the sun is supposed to have brushed off the scar from Scar-face's face and is supposed to be the feather brought down from the sun by Scar-face follow: "Old man says, hand me a feather." The feather is passed to the man. Another song follows: "Old man says he wants a hundred feathers. Old woman wants different kinds of feathers." Seven more songs are sung, the words of some of them are: "This man says that above have seen me. It is powerful. The ground I see is powerful. Old man, says, white buffalo robe I want. Old woman, says, Elk I want. Old man says, don't fool me. Old woman says, don't fool me." The meaning of this is to be sure and give them what they ask for, that is, offerings made at the sun dance to the sun, moon, etc.

Seven songs are sung before they take up the rattles and the rawhide and five songs for the raven. At this time, the man takes hold of one of the rattles by the ball part touching it to the ground, while he holds the end of the handle straight up. The raven songs are: "Raven says, buffalo I am looking for; buffalo I take. The wind is our medicine. The brush is our home. Buffalo I take." The man pecks the rattle handle with one finger on both sides and crows. Then they begin to beat the rattles on the rawhide and shake them in a circle once.

Now seven songs are sung for the smudge which is made of a species of fungus that grows on a kind of willow. The songs: "Old man says, all right, may my lodge be put up. Old woman says, all right may my lodge be put up or built." These words mean that the sun and moon are speaking and want the sun dance lodge built without any accidents.

The next songs are for the natoas bundle which is not opened. The songs: "Old man comes in, he says, I am looking for my bonnet. I have found it. It hears me. It is medicine." The old woman sings and uses the same words in her songs. There are six of these bonnet songs. The songs for the badger skin follow: "The man above hears me; he is powerful. The ground is my home; it is powerful." There are four songs for the badger. The badger skin and other things are not handled, the songs about them are simply sung. The songs for the natoas are: "Old man says I am looking for my bonnet. I have found it: it is powerful." The woman then sings a song with the same words, which is followed by a song about the stone arrow points on the natoas. There is a song for everything which makes up the bonnet which is as follows: the leather band, the blue paint on the band, the stuffed weasel skin tied crosswise on the bonnet, the weasel tails hanging from the bonnet, two feathers in front, and two behind, two plumes on each side of the bonnet, a flint arrow point, a buffalo calf tail, a snipe, and a small doll the head of which is stuffed with tobacco seed. The song for the doll on the bonnet is: "Children are running about. They are running from us. They are running towards us. They are boys. They are powerful." The man says, "Give me the child," and makes the movement of reception. Another song is sung: "Child is crying," and the man imitates the crying of a child. The song for the little birds is: "Bird says water is my medicine; it is powerful," for the calf tail: "Man says calf tail I want," and for the arrow point: "Sharp points are on both sides." Then follows the song for the leather band which represents the lizard: "Yonder man, I am angry and mad at you." This song of the lizard refers to the prairie dog chief. The blue paint on the band represents water and the song for it is: "The blue waters are our medicine." The song for the feathers is: "Feathers I want." Another song for the plume on the feathers:

"Red I want." This closes the evening ceremony. The man and woman are put to bed and all go home.

This is the ceremony after the first sweathouse is made. Three more moves of the entire camp and three more sweathouses must be made. The fourth move and sweathouse is where the sun dance takes place. Nowadays, only one sweathouse is made for the sun dance.

It seems that the final camp is marked out by a society laying rocks around its bounds, according to which the arriving bands find their proper places.

At the fourth camp and on the fourth day, the natoas bundle is opened, or its formal ritual demonstrated. Early in the day another tipi is pitched before the medicine tipi and the covers are joined, thus enlarging the space and providing for a few spectators. A few men and women are invited to assist in the ceremony: the men use the rattles and with the women aid in the singing. The father and other men sit on the north side of the tipi, the former next the medicine woman's husband; and the other women sit on the south side, the mother next to the medicine woman. She directs the medicine woman and the singing of the other women. The ceremony opens at about ten A. M. with the first series of songs in the ritual. Three men hold a rattle in each hand, beating them upon the rawhide by a vigorous downward forward stroke, the seventh rattle is used by the father.

The ritual of the natoas will be found in Volume 7, pp. 215-220. Normally, this ceremony transfers the natoas to the daughter. She may, however, waive the right, in which case the bundle returns to the former owner. Yet, she seems to enjoy all the privileges accorded to one having been an owner.

Theoretically, no one can perform a transfer ceremony without having first owned the bundle in question. In case of the natoas, even now, a beaver owner is regarded as competent to conduct the proceeding, though he may never have gone through the ritual with his wife. This is consistent with the tradition that formerly the natoas was a part of the beaver bundle.[6] Yet, the conditions here are slightly different from those for other bundles in that the father must provide or is charged with the responsibility to see that a natoas is provided. Following the vow, either he or the son makes formal application to the owner of a natoas by the usual presentation of a pipe.[7]

When the daughter begins her fasting, the father has the natoas brought to her tipi. As a rule, the father's wife owns a natoas. Some informants claim that even should the daughter own a natoas, the father must provide another. On the other hand, the daughter can select the eligible natoas. In any case, the father furnishes the daughter with a dress and an elk robe for which he must be paid liberally.[8]

In conclusion, it may be remarked that anyone can make up a natoas, if he has a dream so directing him; also, if he owned a natoas that was lost or otherwise destroyed; if he gave it away, without receiving payment; or if it was buried with someone. Having owned a natoas and transferred it, he cannot duplicate it; should the new owner lose it, he may, if called upon, replace it; likewise, if buried, the surviving husband or wife could call upon

---

[6] In former times, the natoas and the medicine woman's costume were owned by a beaver man. When a woman gave a sun dance she gave a horse for their use. She just borrowed them. Later on, a beaver man transferred them, whence they became a separate bundle.—Tom Kiyo.

[7] Should the woman already own a natoas and the transferrer (father) own one; the woman must say which bundle shall be used. She can use her own, borrow, or purchase of the transferrer.—Curly-bear.

[8] A Piegan informant comments as follows: The woman can either buy or borrow a natoas. In the olden times she often borrowed because the natoas, the dress, the elk tooth wristlets, and the robe were owned by a beaver man's wife. After a time, however, these were transferred to a medicine woman and were thus separated from the beaver bundle.

him. In all such cases fees are given. When one transfers a medicine bundle and has been paid for it, he has no more right to it and cannot duplicate it on his own motion. Should one sell the bundle without the ceremony of transfer, the ritual remains with him and he can again make up the bundle; should one make the transfer and fail to receive the pay, or waive the pay, he can make it up again. The relatives of one buried with a bundle can call upon a former owner to make it up, after which it must be formally transferred to one of them. Men were sometimes killed on the warpath and their bundles lost; such were replaced as noted above. In every case these must be true duplicates; it is only a dream that authorizes new creations, or variations, however slight.

An interesting sidelight is thrown upon the idealized qualities of this woman's function by the following narrative:—

Once while a medicine woman was sleeping in the sacred tipi during the fasting, a nephew of her husband stole in and made improper advances. Being a good and true woman, like all others who give the sun dance, she spurned him. Next day she told her husband the whole story. He was very angry. He was not satisfied with the confession she made, but suspected that she must have given the young man some encouragement. So when all the medicinemen and women had come into the tipi to rehearse the songs as usual, he made a statement of these suspicions and as he had two wives, he proposed to have them change places.

The medicinemen pleaded for the first wife because they believed her innocent, but the husband was obdurate. So the second wife was called in to take the place. Then the first wife said, "It was I who saved this man's life when he was ill. I made the vow to give the sun dance and he got well. I have suffered much in fasting, all for him. Now he disgraces me before all the people. But I will put my virtue to a test. If I am true, I have already acquired power."

She filled a pipe, went outside and standing now on the east side of the tipi, then on the south, the west, and the north, she addressed the sun. The day was clear, but soon after the woman entered the tipi, thunder was heard. A storm came down with hail and blew over many tipis. But in spite of these proofs, her husband was obdurate and the second wife went on with the ceremony.

Not long after the sun dance this same man became ill again. Finally, as a last resort, he called upon the first wife to save him again. This woman told him to call upon the other woman as he seemed to have so much faith in her. So he died and was properly punished for so unjustly treating his faithful wife.

The Procession to the Dancing Lodge.

In our account of the natoas ritual we told how the father, son, etc., emerge from their tipi. The file is headed by the father, followed by the son, next the mother, then the medicine woman followed by women bearing the tongues. The father and the son are muffled in blankets (robes); the latter walks with bowed head, leaning heavily on a staff and bearing over his head a wild rhubarb stalk.[9] The medicine woman wears the natoas on her head, an elkskin (often buckskin) dress and an elkskin robe, with the digging-stick on her back. For a staff, she uses one of the smudge sticks. The women in her rear bear parfleches containing the tongues, together with blankets and other ordinary objects. Two or three old men act as conductors, or flankers, keeping the way clear of spectators, etc. The procession moves slowly and by stages. The four principal personages in it keep their eyes upon the ground. The course is southward past the entrance (east side) to the dancing lodge, around the south side, the rear of the shelter and entering from the north side. Here the medicine woman remains until the dancing lodge is raised at sunset, when she returns to her tipi and breaks her fast with berry soup. The father and the son go to a sweathouse after which their responsibilities also end. During the continuance of the ceremonies in the sun lodge, the medicine woman cares for the natoas bundle, now her property, until transferred to another, but is otherwise free to do as she likes. She usually remains quietly at home receiving guests and resting.

The part of the medicine woman is truly a sacrifice. She and her husband must pay liberally everyone called upon for ceremonial service directly connected with the tongues and the natoas ritual. They must also pay a considerable amount of property for the natoas itself. To give the ceremony means the sacrifice of all

---

[9] Scar-face is said to have made a whistle (flageolet) of such a stalk. The pith of the growing plant is sometimes eaten for food.

personal property. On the other hand, there is compensation, aside from fulfilling the vow. Her relatives are very proud of her since she is so virtuous. She is highly respected by her husband and family. In a measure those who "take the tongues" are also respected. The medicine woman may act as the mother in a future sun dance for which she will receive presents and she may eventually realize something by transferring the natoas to another. Should anything go wrong during the ceremony, the weather be unfavorable, etc., people will look with suspicion upon her and say she must have lied in her confession to the sun. Should she become ill or have deaths in the family, the same charge will be made.

The Offerings of Cloth.

After the procession headed by the father and he is in position at the west side of the dancing lodge, offerings of cloth and clothing are brought up by the people. A man making such an offering hands the father a filled pipe and the cloth. The father holds the pipe and offers prayers for the giver and lights and passes the pipe to other old men sitting around. The cloth he lays in a pile. Then he paints the giver: first the face is smeared over with red, then black spots are daubed on the cheeks, nose, forehead, and chin, four in all. A black circle is marked around each wrist. Women bringing offerings and pipes go to the mother who prays for them and paints their faces red with a black spot on the nose and a black circle around the face. There is also a black circle around each wrist.

The Hundred-Willow Sweathouse.

As stated before, a sweathouse of special form is constructed on the third day. This is said to have originated with Scar-face, it being the house into which he was taken by the sun. About the middle of the day a society is sent out for the willows. These were usually those of the younger men; the pigeons and mosquitoes. There is a belief, however, that in former times only warriors could be sent upon this errand. These persons are mounted and return in procession, singing and circling the medicine woman's tipi in the direction of the sun, and deposit their willows at the west side of the camp circle. They must not drink water while on this duty.

An older society is called to build the sweathouse. They must not drink water while engaged in this operation and receive some of the tongues after the ceremonies of the fourth day. Formerly, these men must have had a coup to their credit as a qualification and some informants claim that the sum total for the society should have totalled at least one hundred, the number of willows. The work begins some time before sunset by which time the sweathouse should be completed.

The willows are stuck into the ground in an oval and their tops bent over and interlocked over the top. The ends point toward the east and the west, an opening or door being provided at each. The willows are then painted, one side red and the other black. Next, a hole is dug in the center of the structure for the heated stones. In the meantime, a small heap of stones mixed with firewood has been placed some distance to the east. A buffalo skull is painted with red spots on one side and black on the other. Sagegrass is thrust into the nose and eye-sockets. Robes are then thrown over the willows and all is ready for the procession from the medicine woman's tipi.

The procession from the medicine woman's tipi consists of the father and another man experienced in ceremonial affairs, the husband, the mother and the medicine woman. They approach slowly and by stages, passing around the south side of the sweathouse to the north and then to the east or entrance. All keep their eyes on the ground. The husband walks with a heavy staff; the medicine woman carries the natoas bundle with a smudge stick.

The men enter the sweathouse, while the two women go to the west side and sit down facing the east. The medicine woman is on the north side with the bundle before her. After the men have entered, the fire is lighted and some of the attendants (builders of the sweathouse) lift the buffalo skull to the top of the sweathouse where it faces the east. Prayers and the usual sweathouse procedure now follow while the stones and a pail of water are passed in by an attendant. The covers are then drawn down and the vapor bath taken.

After the ceremony the procession returns to the medicine woman's tipi. The cover is removed from the sweathouse and the buffalo skull placed on top where it remains.

Should there be more than one medicine woman, another sweathouse is made on the east side of the camp circle and the others grouped around them equally.

Since after the sweathouse ceremony there is formal singing in the tipi until far into the night, it may be said that during the four days of the fast the ceremonies begin with the sweathouse at sundown, while on the fifth day the ceremony begins in the morning and ends at sundown.

To this generalized statement the following account from a Piegan may be added:—

Now, when the first sweathouse is to be made, orders are given in the morning to one of the societies to get the willows to make the hundred-willow sweathouse. Another man is to get the creeping juniper to use in the smudge place in the medicine lodge, and still another is to cut out the smudge place. The moves are short. The people all move camp, as before, and the society goes on ahead and stakes out the camping ground. When the tipis are pitched at the new camping ground, the society comes in with the willows and the rocks for the sweathouse. They circle once around to the right of the lodges and stop outside of the circle, west of the medicine lodge. They must neither eat nor drink while building the sweathouse. They gather wood from among the tipis until they have enough to heat the rocks. Robes for covering the sweathouse are borrowed from the people of the camp. One man goes to the medicine lodge and digs out the smudge place.

When the sweathouse is ready for the medicinemen, four of the men who helped in the construction go and inform the men and women. They carry the parfleche with the tongues in it on a robe, each man holding a corner. The two medicinemen take the lead, the two women follow, then come the four men with the parfleche. Four stops are made before they reach the sweathouse. The instructor leads, and is followed in single file by the other man, and the two women walking very slowly and singing. They march once around the sweathouse in the direction of the sun. The other old men who are to join them and the two medicinemen go in while the two women remain seated on a robe just west of it with the parfleche beside them. A smudge is made with sweetgrass, and a crescent-shaped place marked out between the square hole and the rear of the sweathouse and live coals are placed on the dot in front of the crescent. A song is sung while the smudge stick is taken up and a man goes after the coal for the smudge. The sweetgrass is placed on the live coal and the two songs for the smudge are sung: "Spring grass I take. Where I sit is powerful." A pipe is handed in and the pipe bowl and stem painted red. The man holds the pipe over the smudge and prays for the one who gave it to him and then passes it to the last man to his right who lights it and all smoke it. When the pipe is all burnt out, the man who blessed it, takes it, and with a red-painted stick loosens the ashes and empties some of them on the southeast corner of the square hole in the sweathouse, then on the northwest corner, on the northeast, and finally in the center.

After this the buffalo skull is brought in and the songs of the buffalo sung while the same man paints it with black and red dots, the left half black and the right half in red. Grass is stuffed into the eyes and nose of the skull which is passed out through the west of the sweathouse and placed on the earth taken out of the hole in the sweathouse. An extra buffalo horn wrapped with swamp grass is brought in and given to the man who paints it red and sings while doing so: "Chiefs of other tribes I want to hook." He throws the horn out and all the men of this society who remain near the sweathouse try to catch it. The one who captures it is considered lucky and he is supposed to capture a gun in the next battle he witnesses.

The men in the sweathouse all undress and as they pass their robes and moccasins out through the west of the sweathouse and the door, the buffalo songs are sung. The two medicinemen only wear a robe and moccasins when they go into the sweathouse. While singing, the forked stick is taken up and one of the outsiders goes for the heated stones, stopping four times before he brings them in. One of the men who is inside takes the stone with two straight sticks and places it on the southeast corner of the hole, the same is done with four more stones which are placed on the southwest, the northwest, the northeast corner and the fifth is placed in the bottom of the hole at the center. When a sixth stone is placed in the hole, they are all rolled to the bottom of the hole. Water and a horn spoon or wooden bowl is brought in.

A little water is thrown on the stones to wash them, the curtains are lowered, and prayers to the sun, moon, and stars, and earth begin. In groups of four, sixteen medicine lodge songs are sung. The curtains are raised and four more songs are sung; the sweathouse is opened and four songs are sung, until the sixteen have been completed. The two medicinemen go out through the west of the sweathouse while the rest go through the door. The men dress, and the parfleche containing the tongues is opened and the tongues given to the members of the society who made the sweathouse. The medicinemen and women do not eat. After all are provided with the tongues a piece is broken off each and while all hold the pieces up a prayer is said and the piece of tongue placed on the ground. Then they all begin to eat. After this the robes are all returned to their owners, the buffalo skull placed on top of the frame of the sweathouse with the nose pointed towards the east and the medicinemen and women return in single file while four men follow behind carrying the empty parfleche. The men who belong to the society may now eat and drink as they wish.

The Dancing Lodge.

The dancing lodge may be said to take its origin on the fourth day, by which time the medicine woman has her tipi in place near its site and the camp circle has been formed. In construction, nine forked tree trunks about nine feet in height are set in a circle. Across their tops, except the eastern face, are laid stringers about fifteen feet long of the same material.[10] In the center, is another forked tree trunk much higher than the other (this we shall call the sun pole) connected with each of the stringers by a rafter. Green boughs are placed thickly against the outside of the lodge. On the inside, at the rear, is a booth screened and roofed with boughs. The material is cottonwood. That other woods were occasionally used, is attested by the fact that a locality is known as "the place of sweet pine dancing lodge."

Some informants claim that in former years each band was required to furnish two rafters, a post, a rail, and their

---

[10] Obviously, this would make the dancing lodge very large. In reply to this objection it was said that they were large; that it was necessary to select as a site places where very long rafter poles could be cut; that formerly societies and others performed evolutions within on horseback. The late Little-plume is credited with having introduced the present custom of reciting deeds, requiring horses, outside the dancing lodge. It may be of interest to note that the Arapaho also made very large sun dance shelters.

In 1908 Mr. Duvall measured the dancing lodge. The sun pole stood sixteen feet from the ground to the fork. The posts were eight feet and approximately sixteen feet apart. The diameter of the whole was fifty-two feet. The fireplace was east of the sun pole six feet and was four feet by two feet and five inches deep. The booth for medicinemen was five feet eight inches wide by seven feet six inches deep. The two holes were about a foot forward from the sod walls, eight inches across and six inches deep. The man who has been marking out the site for the lodge during the last few years, begins by selecting the place for the sun pole and stepping off seven paces as the radius.

proportionate amount of boughs. Two rafters were used instead of one as now, each band furnishing the section opposite their place in the circle. The contradiction between the number of bands and the size of the dancing lodge seems not to have troubled our informants. Now, the young men go out during the early part of the fourth day to cut the poles and boughs. This is done without ceremony. A crier usually rides around the camp circle reminding the various bands of their duty. Formerly, the young women went out on horseback to drag in the poles and brush. On this occasion, they dressed in the best costumes and used the finest horse trappings obtainable. The men cut the poles and brush, hitching them to the drag ropes with their own hands. As the procession galloped toward the camp circle, the men rode behind, shooting and yelling. In recent years, the men bring the material in on wagons without demonstration.

Men of some prominence are selected to dig the holes for the posts. The posts are erected and the stringers put in place, excepting one on the west side nearly opposite the entrance. The rafters are leaned against the stringers, ready to be pushed in place and the green boughs piled up at convenient places near by.

The cutting of the sun pole is attended with some ceremony. Some informants claim that formerly this was to be carried out by the medicine woman's band; others that one of the men's societies was called upon for this service. In any event, they go out as a war party and locate a suitable tree. A man with a war record, preferably one having struck an enemy with an ax, comes forward, takes an ax, paints the blade as he recounts some event in which he killed an enemy, and then strikes the tree. Four such deeds must be told before the tree can be felled. Then one or two men cut the tree as the others stand around. As the tree begins to fall all give the war cry and shoot at its top, then rush up, and tearing off branches, wave them in the air as if they were trophies from an enemy. Indeed, the whole proceeding, from start to finish, is a mimic attack on an enemy.

The pole is cut to approximate form and taken to the site of the dancing lodge. One end is placed on a travois (in recent times on a wagon), while the riders assist with their ropes, their horses massed around the travois horse.

The hole for the sun pole is dug without ceremony by relatives of the medicine woman. When it is in place, they tie a bundle of green boughs in the fork,[11] making everything ready for the raising in the evening. The sun pole now lies on the ground with the butt over the hole and the forked end supported by a piece of timber. The fork points to the west. It seems that formerly the pole was painted. Just below the fork it was circled by two black bands and two red ones beneath these.

---

[11] The bundle of boughs is neither spoken of as the thunderbird's nest nor given a name of any kind; though some old men seemed to know that other tribes so designated it. We made diligent inquiry on this point and feel that the above statement is correct. Reference to published photographs will show that the brush is merely gathered into a bundle and not made into the form of a nest as in case of the Crow.

Cutting the Thongs.

A fresh cowskin (formerly two buffalo hides) is provided that thongs may be cut for binding the rafters to the stringers and the objects placed on the sun pole. There seems to have been no hunting ceremony for providing this hide and there is now no symbolic hunting. After the medicine woman is in the shelter, the ceremony of cutting the thongs takes place. If no one volunteers, men are "caught." The men who cut the thongs last year may do the "catching" or engage representatives to do it. Formerly, this function was exercised by old warriors who had captured enemies alive. The "catchers" go quietly about the camp looking for eligibles. While pretending to pass one by without notice, they suddenly lay hold of him. The victim may pull back, but is not allowed to resort to other means of resistance. He is then led up to the hides near the front of the medicine woman's shelter. In former times, four such men were brought up for the ceremony. They must have coups to their records, otherwise they would not have been selected. In the ceremony of 1904 we observed an attempt to "catch" a man on horseback, but the struggles of the horse enabled him to escape. In former times, the friends of the interested party would have gathered around the rear and sides of the horse forcing him forward in the lead of the "catcher". This whole catching procedure is said to symbolize the capture of an enemy.

In order to understand the ceremony that now takes place, it is necessary to know that the right to cut the thong is to the Blackfoot a medicine to be transferred for gifts of property as in case of other medicines. The men who did the cutting in the previous year are to "sell", or transfer, this year. It is they who do the "catching", either in person or by deputy. Should no one be brought forward, those who performed the rite on the previous year must again serve. As soon as a man is caught, his relatives are notified; they come out with all kinds of property to support him in the transfer. The initiate is brought into the presence of the present owner of the right, his hands and face are painted, accompanied by ritualistic prayers. While this proceeds, an old man (usually a relative) stands somewhat apart and shouts out praise for the initiate. However, this may be done by a woman, if no man comes forward. A horse and other property is then given to the former owner of the right, whence it ceases to be his. The deputy "catcher", if there is one, then receives a small present or two from the former owner.

The cutting of the thong then takes place. The new owner of the right, standing up by the hide, shouts out his coups. He holds the knife in his hand and while pointing in different directions with it, he tells of a war deed. At the end of each tale he makes a pass with the knife as if to cut the hide. After four deeds are told, he cuts the hide. For example, he may say, "At such a place I captured a horse which gives me the right to cut this, etc." If there are other men with the right, they follow in turn. After this, the thongs are cut with the assistance of other men and distributed at the places where they will be needed. A thong with the tail attached is used to bind the bunch of boughs to the sun pole, the tail hanging down.

While this ceremony is going on, gifts of flour, beef, etc., made by white people are distributed among the old poor people. This is regarded as a recent intrusion.

The following extract from an unpublished version of the Scarface myth accounts for the thong-cutting ceremony: —

Her husband could tell by her eyes that she had been crying and he said, "I told you not to dig up that turnip, but nevertheless you have done so. Since you are lonesome and wish to return to your people, I will take you back." Then Morningstar went out and killed some buffalo. After he had skinned all of them he cut the hides into long strands, fastened them together, and tied the woman and her child to one end and let her down from the sky to where her people were.

Before she reached the earth, a little sore-eyed boy was lying on his back, looking up at the sky and saw a very small object coming down. The boy told the men who were playing the wheel gambling game what he saw, but they laughed at him and threw dirt in his eyes and said, "You must see the gum on your eyelids or lashes." As the falling object came closer others noticed it and when it came among the group they knew that it was the woman who was missing from the camp. They untied the rawhide strand and noticed that some of the buffalo tails were on the ends of the long rope which lay piled up high before them.

This woman came down with her digging-stick. As she was not a wicked woman and only lived with Morningstar as her husband, she gave her digging-stick to the medicine lodge woman and the natoas was named for the turnip she dug up. When the sun dance was held, this woman told them always to cut up a rawhide into strands and tie the posts with them. Also that the center post and the birch on it must be tied with them. The tail of the hide is to hang down from the center post. These rawhide strands are a representation of the rawhide rope with which this woman was let down to the earth. Later, the moose hoofs are tied to this digging-stick. The plumes on the natoas are to represent the leaf of the large turnip this woman dug up while in the sky.

Raising the Sun Pole.

While the hide is being cut, all the woman who made vows to take some of the tongues come forward to the parfleche placed near the medicinemen and women. Each woman takes one of the tongues and stands with the person for whom her vow was made and makes a confession to the sun in a loud voice, so all may hear. Then she prays to the sun for the beneficiary. After all the women have taken their tongues, some of the men tie the cloth offerings to the ends of the poles and a bunch of birch is tied between the forks of the center pole.

The preceding ceremony comes to a close as the sun gets very low. About time for the sun to set, a procession of pole raisers starts from each of the four quarters of the camp circle. Tipi poles are tied near the small ends in pairs, each pair carried by two men. The four parties advance in unison by four stages and at each pause sing a special song. In the last move, they rush upon the sun pole and raise it in place. In the meantime, the father and son go and stand on the center pole while their wives stand to the west. The men make wing movements with their arms toward the east. According to some informants, the medicine woman may make hooking motions at the pole, to symbolize the mythical Elk-woman.

Four men are called upon to assist the father and son. As the latter stand upon the pole, they encircle and screen them with their blankets and join the father in singing. The songs call for good luck in erecting the dancing lodge. The son does not sing. Four songs are sung. At the end of each the father blows a whistle while someone shakes the pole. The last time they jump off the pole. The son drops his blanket (some say the father also, some add moccasins) painted black as a sun offering. Another blanket is handed him at once.

As soon as the men leave the pole the advancing raisers rush in, raise the center pole, put on the rafters, tie them with the rawhide strands and place brush all around to form the wind-break. This is accompanied by much shouting, but without shooting.

While the sun pole is being raised the daughter and mother stand watching it. They pray and make movements with the corners of their robes as though steering the rising pole. As it sways from side to side, they gesture as if righting it.

As soon as the pole is set, the natoas, robe, and moccasins are taken off the daughter by the mother. She may call on someone to do this and pay a gun or a horse for the service. The mother and other attendants then lead the daughter to her tipi where she resumes her ordinary routine.

The father and son go to a sweathouse where all the paint is washed off. This is not the hundred-willow sweathouse and is the fifth sweathouse, if it were counted. The two men go in and some sagegrass being handed to the father, he takes off the feathers tied to the son's hair, the hair necklace, and whistle. After the first opening of the sweathouse he takes the sagegrass and wipes off the black paint on the son and hands out through the west side of the sweathouse the necklace, whistle, and feathers which are to be taken home. At the same time, the two women are in the ceremonial lodge, the mother caring for the daughter.

When the men have completed the sweathouse ceremony they go to the medicine woman's tipi. The father and his wife wrap up the natoas and place it in the badger skin. After this is done, they no longer have to eat sparingly. This ends the ceremony of the medicine woman.

Early the next day she and her husband must obtain the cottonwood brush with which the booth for the weather dancers is made. Another man digs out the place in the booth, making it the same as the smudge place in the medicine woman's tipi, with the sod on three sides and creeping juniper on top of it. The fireplace is dug out to the west of the center post and is made as in the medicine woman's tipi. When going for and returning the brush, the woman rides one horse and leads the one dragging her travois. While when the other brush was brought in there was much shooting and shouting, there are now no demonstrations of any kind, but absolute silence.

The Weather Dancers.

Early on the fifth day, a booth is built inside the dancing lodge opposite the entrance. A slight excavation about six feet square is made over which is erected a shelter of green cottonwood boughs, open on the side facing the sun pole. Before the middle of the day, a procession of one or more men supposed to have power over the weather, attended by drummers, proceeds by stages from the medicine woman's tipi to this booth. They pause four times and dance, facing alternately the east and the west. They hold whistles of bone in their mouths, which are sounded in unison with the dancing. The procession is of two transverse lines, the dancers, in front, the drummers and singers behind. A great deal of dancing is done between the entrance to the dancing lodge and the booth. At intervals during the day they stand before the booth and dance to the east and west: the drummers are now stationed on the south side of the booth where women also assemble for the singing. The dancing is chiefly an up and down movement produced by flexing the knees, the eyes are directed toward the sun and wing-like movements of the hands are made in the same direction. The dancers wear breechcloth and moccasins and usually a robe around the waist. Their faces and bodies are painted according to their own medicines and medicine objects worn on their heads.

It is stated that there is but one weather dancer, but others may join under certain conditions. In practice this seems to amount to there being a director or leader in the dance, at least such was the case in 1903 and 1904. In 1904 the two assistant dancers went to the medicine woman's tipi to paint themselves and began their procession from there, while the leader approached in a similar manner from his own tipi, the two forming one procession before the east side of the dancing lodge was reached. The leading dancer wore a special ceremonial robe, headdress, and several medicine objects, which have been described in Volume 7 (pp. 98-99).

These objects and their medicine functions may be regarded as esoteric in so far as they are not absolutely essential to the office of leading dancer. Yet, this same individual seems to have performed this function for a number of years. Clark mentions strings of feathers tied to the finger of this dancer.[12]

In 1904 there were two assistant dancers. Both wore headdresses somewhat like that of their leader. One was fully dressed with a blanket around his waist; the other was nude to the belt. The latter was painted chiefly in red with a circle in blue on the back and one on the breast. The former had a pair of horizontal lines on each cheek, those on the right, black, on the left, red.

It is said that formerly these dancers were nude, except for the breechcloth and moccasins. The entire body was painted. There seemed to have been no fixed painting, but the sun, moon, and stars were usually represented. Around the head, they wore a wreath of juniper and bands of sagegrass around the neck, wrists, and ankles.

The weather dancers are not permitted to eat or drink during the day. Formerly, they remained in the booth continuously until the evening of the fourth day of their dancing; in recent years, they spend the night at home and return to the booth in the morning.

The functions of these dancers are not clearly understood. They seem to be held responsible for the weather: i. e., upon them falls the duty of preventing rain from interfering with the dancing. Whether they do this because they happen to have independent shamanistic powers or whether it is a mere function of their temporary office in the ceremony, cannot be determined. Other medicinemen often attempt to control the weather during the days preceding the formal entry into the booth as well as during the later days. In 1903 (Piegan) there was a contest between a

---

[12] Clark, W. P., *The Indian Sign Language* (Philadelphia, 1885), 72.

number of rival medicinemen some of whom conjured for rain, others for fair weather: strange to say, clouds would threaten and then pass away during these days, which coincidence was interpreted as proof of evenly matched powers. Several times one of the partisans of fair weather came out near the site of the dancing lodge and danced to the sun, holding up a small pipe and occasionally shouting. He wore no regalia and danced in a different manner from that observed among the weather dancers at the booth. However, the man who led the weather dancers for many years until his death in 1908, was famous for his control over the weather. Once, it is told, he became enraged at the power making the weather bad, shouting out "Now, you go ahead, if you want to. I have great power and can stop you when I will."

In former times, the dreams of the weather dancers while sleeping in the booth were considered of special supernatural significance, since, it is said, they were *en rapport* with the sun. This *rapport* may account for what seems to be one of their chief functions—blessing the people. During the days they are in the booth, individuals come to them "to be prayed for." They come up and stand before the booth. The dancer takes black paint and paints their faces. Then he prays to the sun for their welfare. During this part of the ceremony the recipient faces the sun. Again, the medicine-pipes and other ritualistic objects are brought up for the dancer to present to the sun. The pipes he holds up with the stems towards the sun, whom he addresses at some length, offering him a smoke, making requests, etc., after which he smokes the pipe. All the persons present are then permitted to put their lips to the pipe from which they are supposed to derive great benefits. The dancer also receives offerings made to the sun. A young man may fill a pipe and approach with his offerings. The dancer takes the pipe, smokes, prays, paints the man's face, and makes the offering. A woman or child may do this; or a whole family. Formerly, a great deal of old clothing was offered at this time, a custom still practised by the Blood. Also children's moccasins and clothing were offered in this way. As they grew out of them they were given to the sun to promote well-being. In last analysis, it seems that while these dancers are spoken of as weather priests, they are rather sun priests, since through them appeals to the sun are made. It should be noted that they are regarded as independent of and in no way associated with the medicine woman ceremonies or the erection of the dancing lodge, but upon entrance to the booth, the leading weather dancer is said to become the chief and director of all succeeding ceremonies. The length of the ceremony depends entirely upon him and formerly continued as long as he kept his place.

Like other rites this one was bought and sold, but it was usual to continue in ownership many years. Anyone could make a vow to dance with the weather dancer and join him in his ceremonies, but such vows were usually made by former owners of the rite. When one makes a vow to purchase the rite, its owner must sell, however reluctant he may be. The transfer must be in the sun dance. It is said that two men once alternately sold to each other for many years so that both could appear in every sun dance.

Dancing.

The first ceremony of this character is named the cutting-out dance (to cut out a hole in a robe). It seems to have been performed by a society and occurs early on the fifth day. About four or six old men dance in line with a rawhide which they hold in front of them, singing and beating time on the rawhide with rattles similar to those of the beaver men. The society now divides into two parties, one placing itself north of the center pole, and the other party standing in line south of the center pole. The two parties dance back and forward in front of the pole shooting at it. The old men on the west side of the center pole dance in their places. The rawhide held in front of them, hangs down like an apron. They beat time on it, holding the rawhide in one hand, and the rattles in the other. An old man counts deeds and marks out with a knife the fireplace and the booth for the weather dancers. These are dug while the dancing and shooting take place.[13]

The hole, or fire pit, is dug between the sun pole and the entrance to the dancing lodge. It is about three feet by two and "two hands" deep. A warrior is then called to start the fire. Warriors now come forward in turn to count their coups. In this a man took a piece of firewood and holding it up, called out in a loud voice how he once struck a Sioux, a Snake, etc., then placed it in the fire. When he had recounted all he gave way to the next. Stories are told of men having enough coups to make a fire large enough to threaten the destruction of the dancing lodge. We were

---

[13] It will be recalled that in the sun dance of the Dakota type (p. 110) there is a ceremonial shooting at the sun pole. Here the shooting takes place in a perfunctory way, while the pole is dragged to the sun dance site. Yet, McQuesten claims to have witnessed the driving of evil power from the sun lodge at a Blood ceremony in 1912. ("The Sun Dance of the Blackfeet" *Rod and Gun in Canada*, March 1912.) As this is not noted in older accounts and we failed to get information as to it, we suspect it to be due to foreign influences, or perhaps the author's own interpretation.

able to confirm the statement of Clark[14] that the height of the flame as determined by a buffalo tail hanging down was the criterion for determining a great warrior. One informant states as follows:—

There is always a cow tail hanging down from the center post. In olden times this was a buffalo tail, to the end of which a blackened plume was tied. This hangs down over the fireplace which was used at night to furnish light for the proceedings. The assembled people were entertained by narratives of warriors as they came forward to narrate their deeds; each threw a stick on the fire for each deed counted and he whose fire blazed high enough to reach the tail was considered a great warrior. It was a great honor when a man could tell enough war deeds to scorch the tail. All this time there was singing (the cheering songs) and drumming, while berry soup was served to all. The persons taking part are designated as those "who are about to make the fire." In recent years, this ceremony has been performed in a very perfunctory manner.

After the ceremony, the fire was fed in the ordinary way and kept going during the greater part of the succeeding days. The origin of this dance is often ascribed to Scar-face.

---

[14] Clark, *ibid.*, 72.

Society Dances.

In former times, the succeeding days were apportioned to the men's societies (the ikunukats) in the order of their rank, beginning at the lowest.[15] There seems to have been no fixed allotment of time to each, only the order of succession being adhered to. The ceremonies were determined chiefly by the respective society rituals, though the recounting of deeds in war was given great prominence. As a rule, each society closed its ceremonies by offering parts of its regalia, etc., to the sun, a custom still observed by the Blood (See vol. II, this series, fig. 19, p. 411). After the highest society had completed its function, the leading men of the tribe held a kind of a war dance in which coups were recounted. In this dance, again, rattles were beaten upon a rawhide. The organizations or persons having charge of the day's ceremonies must furnish the feast and all necessaries. The medicine woman and her husband usually repair to the dancing lodge each day. The man usually takes his pipe and tobacco and furnishes the smoking for the guests who sit around. His wife wears the buckskin dress and elk robe, but not the natoas. They sit on the north or right side of the booth and merely are spectators. This closes the ceremonies and camp is broken.

---

[15] This series, Vol. II, 365-474.

The Torture Ceremony.

The torture feature, especially prominent in the ceremonies of the Mandan, Hidatsa, and Dakota, was formerly given a place among the dancing lodge ceremonies of the Blackfoot. The information we have seems to indicate that this ceremony had not become thoroughly adjusted to its place in this series at the time of its prohibition by the United States and Canadian governments. The claim is made by some of the Piegan that it was borrowed from the Arapaho and was not looked upon with much favor. As one man expressed it, "None of those taking the cutting lived to reach old age." It was said that a few Blackfoot warriors once visited the Arapaho at the time of their sun dance where they were put through the cutting ceremony. According to the Blackfoot mode of thought, this means that the medicine rites (and rights) were transferred to them. When they returned, they induced others to take the cutting, to whom, of course, the rites were transferred. Whether this historical statement is accurate or mythical, we have no means of knowing, but we are inclined to give it some weight as evidence. It seems, however, that warriors took the cutting because of a vow, similar to that of the medicine woman. Sometimes a man dreamed that the sun required it of him. The giving of property and the conditions of the transfer were the same as for "cutting the thong," though we have no information that "catching" was permitted. Such may, however, have been tolerated.

The men taking the cutting were nude to the belt. Sage was tied around the wrists and ankles. The hair hung down, held in place by a wreath of cedar (some informants say sage). They were painted white. Rows of spots in blue extended down the sides of the face, over the shoulders and down the arms. Wavy lines of the same color were also drawn down the arms. A circle representing the sun, was made on the breast, also upon the chin and probably on the back opposite the one over the heart. On the forehead was another circle representing the moon. Other informants say a crescent moon in black was used instead of these circles.

According to one informant, vows were made to purchase this ceremony when ill or in great danger. If the promise brought results, the vow was fulfilled at the next dance. The supplicant calls upon one having purchased the rite. They enter the booth of the weather dancers, a blanket is held up to shut out the gaze of the others. The transferrer then paints the purchaser. He cuts a hole through the skin of the right shoulder, over the scapula, and a hole over each breast. A small sharpened stick is thrust through each. A shield is hung on the back. Long cords were fastened to those on the breast, the ends of which were tied fast, high up to the center pole. The purchaser goes up to the pole, embraces it, and cries for a time. Then he backs off, and dancing, throws his weight on the ropes. The transferrer jerks the shield from his shoulders and if necessary, assists him in tearing loose. At once, the purchaser goes out into the hills and sleeps in different places to receive power.

It is said that all who take this ceremony die in a few years, because it is equivalent to giving one's self to the sun. Hence, the sun takes them for his own.

The cutting was similar to that described by Catlin and other writers as observed elsewhere. Some informants say the dancers held whistles in their mouths and gazed at the sun as they danced. When all the thongs were torn out, some of the lacerated flesh was cut off as an offering to the sun.

McLean reports the following observations upon this ceremony at a Blood sun dance:—

... The chief attraction to the pale-face is what has been ignorantly termed "making braves." I desired very much to see this ceremony *once*, that I might know the facts from personal observation, and draw my own conclusions after conversing with the Indians.

Two young men having their whole bodies painted, wearing the loin-cloth only, and with wreaths of leaves around their heads, ankles and wrists, stepped into the center of the lodge. A blanket and a pillow were laid on the ground, and one of the young men stretched himself upon them. As he lay, an old man came forward and stood over him and then in an earnest speech told the people of the brave deeds, and noble heart of the young man. In the enumeration of his virtues and noble deeds, after each separate statement the musicians beat applause. When the aged orator ceased, the young man arose, placed his hands upon the old man's shoulders, and drew them downward, as a sign of gratitude for the favorable things said about him. He lay down, and four men held him while a fifth made the incisions in his breast and back. Two places were marked in each breast denoting the position and width of each incision. This being done, the wooden skewers being in readiness, a double edged knife was held in the hand, the point touching the flesh, a small piece of wood was placed on the under side to receive the point of the knife when it had gone through, and the flesh was drawn out the desired length for the knife to pierce. A quick pressure and the incision was made, the piece of wood was removed, and the skewer inserted from the under-side as the knife was being taken out. When the skewer was properly inserted, it was beaten down with the palm of the hand of the operator, that it might remain firmly in its place. This being done to each breast, with a single skewer for each, strong enough to tear away the flesh, and long enough to hold the lariats fastened to the top of the sacred pole, a double incision was made on the back of the left shoulder, to the skewer of which was fastened an Indian drum. The work being pronounced good by the persons engaged in the operation, the young man arose, and one of the operators fastened the lariats giving them two or three jerks to bring them into position.

The young man went up to the sacred pole, and while his countenance was exceedingly pale, and his frame trembling with emotion, threw his arms around it, and prayed earnestly for strength to pass successfully through the trying ordeal. His prayer ended he moved backward until the flesh was fully extended, and placing a small bone whistle in his mouth, he blew continuously upon it a series of short sharp sounds, while he threw himself backward, and danced until the flesh gave way and he fell. Previous to his tearing himself free from the lariats, he seized the drum with both hands and with a sudden pull tore the flesh on his back, dashing the drum to the ground amid the applause of the people. As he lay on the ground, the operators examined his wounds, cut off the flesh that was hanging loosely, and the ceremony was at an end. In former years the head of a buffalo was fastened by a rope on the back of the person undergoing the feat of self-immolation, but now a drum is used for that purpose.

From two to five persons undergo this torture every Sun-Dance. Its object is military and religious. It admits the young man into the noble band of warriors, whereby he gains the esteem of his fellows, and opens up the path to fortune and fame. But it is chiefly a religious rite. In a time of sickness, or danger, or in starting upon some dangerous expedition, the young man prays to Natos for help, and promises to give himself to Natos if his prayers are answered. Upon his return, when the Annual Sun-Dance is held, he fulfills his vow, gives himself to his god, and thus performs a twofold duty. Of course the applause of the people and the exhibition of courage are important factors in this rite, but its chief feature is a religious one. Instead of being a time of feasting and pleasure, the Sun-Dance is a military and religious festival, in connection with which there are occasions for joy, and the feast enhances the pleasure.[16]

---

[16] McLean, John, "The Blackfoot Sun Dance" (*Proceedings of the Canadian Institute*, third series, vol. 6, Toronto, 1888), 235-237.

It may be well to note that the offering of bits of flesh to the sun was a general practice not necessarily associated with the sun dance. Many comparatively young men now living (1904) bear numerous scars testifying to such offerings. When in perilous situations a finger would sometimes be struck off with a call upon the sun for help. Among the Blood, such sacrifice of a finger by women as well as men was common at the sun dance.[17] These facts concerning the more general practice of mutilating the body to win the approval of the sun suggest that if the cutting ceremony is intrusive, it either found on hand a series of analogous customs or brought with it a concept that afterwards gave birth to them. It may be observed that the form of costume and dance is strikingly like that employed by the present weather dancers.

Since there seems to be no good published data on the sacrificing of skin and fingers we append the narrative of Split-ears:—

Sometimes, when warriors are on an expedition and come in sight of the enemy they will sit in a circle while the leader, or the oldest member of the party, offers prayers that they may succeed in their undertaking. Then they proceed to offer bits of their own skin to the sun. The one who prayed sits down by one of the party, takes

---

[17] McLean, as an eye-witness to such a sacrifice, gives the following:—

"As I stood outside the lodge, a young Indian friend of mine, went to an old medicine-woman and presented his sacrifice to Natos. During the year he had gone on a horse-stealing expedition and as is customary on such occasions had prayed to Natos for protection and success, offering himself to his god if his prayers were answered. He had been successful and he now presented himself as a sacrifice. The old woman took his hand held it toward the Sun and prayed, then laying a finger on a block of wood she severed it with one blow from a knife and deer's horn scraper. She held the portion of the finger cut off toward the Sun and dedicated that to him as the young man's sacrifice." (p. 235.)

up a needle or bodkin and a knife, thrusts the former under a small section of skin and raising it, cuts off a small slice with a knife. This leaves a circular wound a quarter of an inch or less in diameter. It is understood that the operator pulls the skin up with the needle and slices off a small section underneath that instrument. He then takes up some black paint and dips the bit of skin into it. Then he holds it up to the sun and prays for the success of his victim. The bit of skin is then placed upon a piece of cloth and another is removed from the victim in the same manner and so the operator goes to each of the party in turn, each time removing a piece of skin, dipping it in black paint, and holding it up in a prayer to the sun. While each person is expected to give two pieces, they are not limited to the maximum number, some men giving four and some still more. The bits of skin thus collected are tied up in one corner of the cloth which is mounted upon a stick wrapped with wild sage, the whole being fastened in a tree or set up on the top of a high hill as the sun's offering. This sacrifice is always spoken of as feeding the sun with flesh from one's own body. The cloth is fastened to the stick in the form of a flag or banner so that it waves in the wind with the flesh offerings tied in one corner. This sacrifice is considered one of the greatest a man can make.

Now, as I have said, some men only give two small pieces of skin, while others give a great many more, but as they do this each time they go on an expedition, it so happens that a man who made many war expeditions has many small scars on his arms and legs. Thus, we can still tell those of our old men who went upon the warpath many times in their youth. We can tell by the scars made from feeding the sun their own flesh. But, again, it so happens that men while at home may have dreams in which they are commanded to feed the sun. Now it is believed that unless a man heeds such a command, he is certain to be visited by misfortune or even death, so he always makes haste to comply with the command. After such a dream he makes a sweathouse and invites in an old man who prays and makes the offering. The procedure here is the same as previously described and the offering is made into a banner and placed in a tree or upon a hill. Then again, the men who are at home in the camp but who have relatives in a war party may so wish for the safety of these that they themselves offer bits of skin in their behalf. Thus, you see, there are many times when people will offer bits of skin, so that it was not uncommon for a man to have one hundred or more scars upon his body. These are generally arranged in rows up and down the arms, down the legs, down the breasts and the back. I have even heard of cases where a man is said to have offered one hundred pieces of skin at one time. This, however, was unusual.

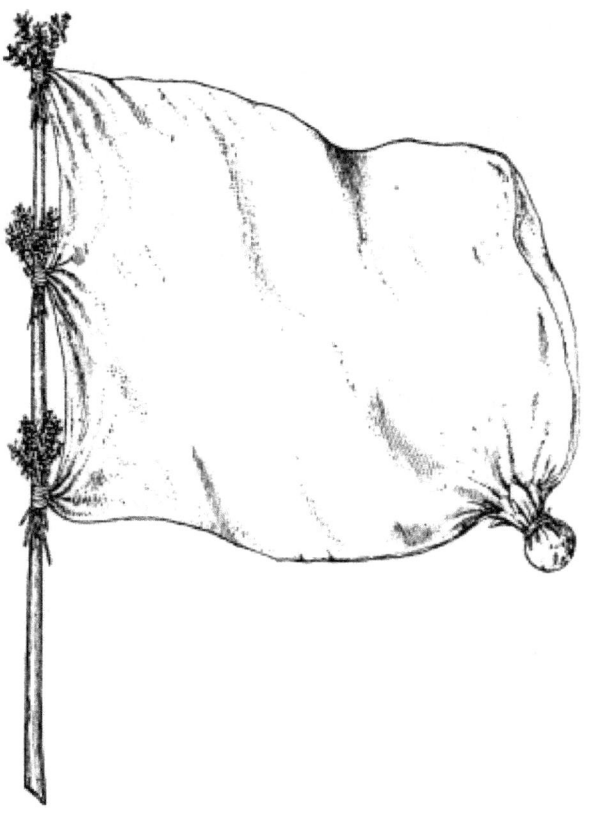

Fig. 1. The Offering of Human Flesh. The bits of flesh are tied in the corner of the banner. Drawn from a native sketch.

Sometimes, instead of offering skin, the warrior would offer a finger. Thus, if beset by very great danger on the warpath a man may make a vow to the sun stating that if brought home safely he will sacrifice a finger. This sacrifice can be made at any time; either when on the warpath or when at home in camp or at the sun dance. In such cases, the finger is offered to the sun in the precise manner as the pieces of skin described above.

There are, however, occasions upon which fingers are cut off that are not offerings to the sun. Thus, people who are in mourning sometimes sacrifice a finger. In those cases it is usual to call upon some old woman who is skilled in the amputation. She cuts off the finger, usually reciting a kind of ritual, but it is not offered to the sun. It is simply thrown away. Then again babies' fingers are sometimes cut off to give the child good luck. Thus, if a woman lost many children she would call upon an old woman to make the sacrifice for her newly born. In this case, the tip end of a finger is cut off and wrapped up in a piece of meat which the mother is required to swallow. This is supposed to insure the child's living to maturity. It had no connection with the sun.

I have told you how men are called upon to cut off pieces of skin and how certain old women were selected to amputate fingers. You should also know that in olden times there were some women and men who might be called upon to cut open dead persons for various reasons. Sometimes they did this on their own account in order to get information as to the cause of death.

These accounts show for one thing that the cutting ceremony in the sun dance is but one of a type of blood and flesh offerings made to the sun, in fulfillment of a vow. The sacrifice of a finger is more frequent and less specialized, though frequently done at the sun dance. Then comes the very frequent offering of bits of skin, a sacrifice common in war raids at all times. The offering of bits of skin in the precise manner described here is found elsewhere in the Plains. The writer has observed men so scarred among several divisions of the Dakota. The method of removing the skin was here the same as followed by the Blackfoot. The thrusting in of the awl has a curious similarity to the cutting and skewering in the sun dance; one may even be pardoned for wondering if it did not so arise.

Sun Dance Songs.

Two songs have a special place in the ceremony. They are sung by the men as they ride into camp with the willows for the hundred-willow sweathouse. They are sung again when the procession of pole raisers moves up to raise the sun pole. Formerly, they were sung by any considerable body of the tribe approaching the camp of strange Indians. Likewise, when they approached a post to open trade.[18]

Red-plume, a Piegan, has a smudge stick on which are notches said to represent the number of different songs used in the ceremonies of the medicine woman. There are 413 which is said to be the full number of songs. These, as has been stated in Volume 7, are in reality a part of the beaver bundle ritual.

The singing at the dancing ceremonies after the sun lodge has been erected is usually confined to the songs of various societies concerned. There are, however, a few with characteristic airs that are regarded as peculiarly appropriate to the occasion, regardless of who may be dancing.

---

[18] For musical notation see McClintock, Walter, *The Old North Trail, or Life, Legends and Religion of the Blackfoot Indians* (London, 1910), 311.

The Sun Dance Camp.

In a previous paper, we called attention to the belief that the camp circle was formed expressly for the sun dance. Our informants say that formerly the circle was formed by the assemblage of the bands some time before the medicine woman began her fast. In winter, the tribes scattered out, usually two to five bands in a camp, often many miles apart. At the approach of summer, the husband of a woman having made a vow to give the sun dance sends a man to look up the camps and invite them to join his band. He carries tobacco and presents some to each head man with the invitation. As the head men receive the invitation, they order their bands to move, forming the circle at the medicine woman's camp. Once formed, the circle is not broken until after the sun dance, a period estimated at from two to four months. The whole body may move about and even make long journeys aside from the four ceremonial moves required while the medicine woman is fasting. After the sun dance, they split up into parties for the fall hunt and finally went into winter quarters. The import of our former statement is thus apparent. The suggestion is that the camp circle is intimately associated with the sun dance. At least, one point is clear, the camp circle is initiated by the woman who starts the sun dance and even so is one of the preparatory steps.

As previously stated in Volume 7 of this series, there is much uncertainty as to the order of bands in the circle. We doubt if it ever was absolutely fixed beyond change at the will of those in charge of the sun dance proceedings.

Mythological Notes.

The way that several distinct myths are used to account for different features of the sun dance might be taken as a suggestion that the ceremony grew up among the Blackfoot. We suspect, however, that we have here an example of pattern phenomena. Those familiar with the detailed study of rituals in Volume 7 will recall that tradition recognized the obvious fact that rituals were not produced all at once, but grew by accretions. This is so marked in the mythical accounts of ritual origin that we may suspect its appearance in the mythology of the sun dance. On page 241 we have enumerated the myths accounting for important features of the ceremony. Among these are not included the parts taken by societies or the cutting sacrifices, they, as we have stated, not being regarded as integral parts of the sun dance.

For the sake of completeness we offer some extracts from an unpublished version of the Scar-face myth:—

We will take up this narrative at the point where Scar Face has killed the cranes and reported with their scalps. We are told that had not Scar Face killed these birds, they would always have killed people, but that since he overpowered them they now fear people and have done so ever since.

Now, the Sun, the Moon, Scar Face, and Morningstar had a scalp dance while the Sun and Moon sang the praise songs in honor of Scar Face. The Sun addressed Scar Face: "When your people kill enemies they should scalp them and then give a scalp dance. Whenever anyone counts coup or recounts his war experiences, the praise songs should be sung." We have followed this custom ever since. Whenever anyone related his war deeds, some old men or old woman sang the praise songs, repeating the narrator's name during the singing.

The Sun was pleased with Scar Face. He directed Morningstar and Scar Face to build four sweathouses, standing side by side, with their entrances facing east. When they were completed, the Sun, Morningstar, and Scar Face entered one of them, the Moon remaining outside to close the door. After the Sun had worked over Scar Face, he ordered the moon to open the door and they went into the next sweathouse, again choosing the moon to be the door attendant. Now, the Sun asked the Moon to point out her son. The Moon designated Morningstar. They moved into the third sweathouse where the Sun had Morningstar and Scar Face exchange seats. Again, the Moon was asked to pick out her son. Though she noticed that the scar on the young man's face had disappeared, she pointed to her own son. They proceeded to the fourth sweathouse. Again, the Sun had the two men exchange places. The Moon looked in and pointing to Scar Face said, "This is Morningstar." The Sun replied, "You have mistaken him for Morningstar, the other is our son." Ever since that time, Scar Face has always been called Mistaken Morningstar.

Then the Sun gave Scar Face a buckskin suit decorated with porcupine quills. On the breast and back of the shirt were quill-worked rosettes representing the sun; the side seams of the leggings and sleeves were covered with strips of quillwork three or four inches wide. In addition, the sleeves and leggings bore hair fringes representing the scalps of cranes killed by Scar Face. The Sun also gave Scar Face a bow with a lock of hair fastened to one end, a whistle made of a hollow reed, a bladder, and the robe worn by Scar Face. To represent the scalping, the Sun painted the upper part black. The whistle and the bladder were to be used on the woman who had refused Scar Face. The bow too, is a reminder of the killing of the cranes and is still used in the sun dance lodge. The Sun gave Scar Face a circle of creeping juniper which the women that build the lodge (the sun dance or medicine lodge) are to wear on their heads.

The Sun told Scar Face of the sun dance, the lodge, and the sweathouse, and added, "When you return to your people and wish to make an offering to me, you must first build a sweathouse and there make your offerings. Then I will hear your prayers and accept them. You may also make offerings to me in the sun dance lodge." He covered Scar Face's face with the "seventh" or red paint, drew a black circle around his face and a black dot on the bridge of his nose, and a streak of black around each wrist. He said to Scar Face, "This is the way the people must paint when they make offerings to me in the sun dance lodge. For the victory or scalp dance they must paint their faces black." The Sun also gave him a necklace, in the center of which were strung two small shells and a pendent lock of hair, flanked on either side by four beads. This is the necklace worn by the husband of the woman owning the natoas. The Sun's lodge was made of white buffalo robes and some the color of beaver skins. The door of the Sun's lodge faced the east. For this reason, tipis were always turned so the doors faced east. Now Scar Face decided to return to the place where Spider waited.

The narrative then proceeds in the usual way, except that the hero calls all the men of the camp to take revenge on the young woman after which he by magic turns her into a cripple.

The Blood and North Blackfoot.

The writer has upon two occasions seen the ground where a Blood sun dance had been held. The dancing lodge, the sweathouse, etc., were still standing and all these were just as noted among the Piegan. The Blood lodge was a little larger, but the Piegan said that it was formerly so with them, they now having very poor timber to work with. We have in addition two brief published accounts of eyewitnesses.[19] The chief difference we could detect was in the secondary dances of the society where the Horns and the Matoki[20] took a very prominent part. As there are now no such organizations among the Piegan, this gives merely an outward appearance of difference.

The Northern Piegan, as may be expected, also had the same form. As to the North Blackfoot, we have only the statement of other Indians that the sun dance was the same. The Sarsi[21] also had the very same form and we may suspect the Kutenai as well. At least, my Piegan informants asserted that the Kutenai had the sun dance from them. The problem here, however, must rest until we have more data, though Hale is of the opinion that the Blackfoot gradually displaced the Kutenai and took over many Plains traits from them.[22]

---

[19] McLean, *ibid.*, 231-237; McQuesten, *ibid.*, 1169-1177.
[20] This series, volume II, 410-418, 430-435.
[21] Goddard, Pliny Earle, "Sarsi Texts" (*University of California Publications in American Archaeology and Ethnology*, vol. 11, no. 3, Berkeley, 1915), 192-195.
[22] Hale, H., "On the North-Western Tribes of Canada" (*Report, Fifty-seventh Meeting, British Association for the Advancement of Sciences*, 173-200, London, 1888), 198.

www.ingramcontent.com/pod-product-compliance
Lightning Source LLC
Chambersburg PA
CBHW060503110426
42738CB00055B/2603